MUSIC THERAPY

Poems by
Peter Olds

Earl of Seacliff Art Workshop
Paekakariki
2001

c. Peter Olds, 2001

Other books by Peter Olds

Lady Moss Revived (Caveman 1972)
Freeway (Caveman 1974)
Doctor's Rock (Caveman 1976)
Beethoven's Guitar (Caveman 1980)
After Looking For Broadway (One Eyed Press 1985)

Acknowledgments are due to the following publications where some of the poems in this book first appeared: **Takahe, Glottis, & Litter** (O.U.S.A. Review.)

Cover photo - Peter Olds
Back cover photo - Billy Lawry

Special thanks to: Clare O'Leary, Cathy Ellis, Sue Apperley
& Martin Schaenzel

Music Therapy is published by:

Earl of Seacliff Art Workshop
P.O. Box 42
Paekakariki

ISBN 1-86942-023-3

Published with the assistance of Creative New Zealand

Notes

* Mount Charlotte was named after Matron Charlotte Beswick by Doctor Truby King, Superintendent of Seacliff Mental Hospital, 1889-1920.
* The museum mentioned has been shifted to Dunedin & is now housed in the Early Settlers Museum.
* Most of the rubble & bricks from the main Hospital buildings were bulldozed across Russell Road to 'cow gully swamp' in the 1950s. All of the Seacliff district is still littered with the hospital's body parts.
Clifton House has since been demolished.
Cherry Farm is closed & there are no more helicopter rides.
* Karla Tucker was executed in Texas USA on Feb 3rd 1998 for the pick-axe murder of her ex-lover. While in prison she became a born-again Christian & married the prison chaplain. She was fourteen years on death row.
* On Majoribanks Street, Wellington, there was a coffee bar called The Intermezzo in the 1960s.
* Onetangi Beach has probably been sold.

The poems in this collection were written after a long illness.

Special thanks to Juanita & Bryan for the use of a small hut on Russell Road, Seacliff.

To the memory of Janet, the hen.

Go to the pine if you want to learn about the pine or to the bamboo if you want to learn about the bamboo.

- Basho

Contents

I
Uncovering the Hospital

Letter from Seacliff	6
Uncovering the Hospital	7
Superintendent's Garden	13
From a Grove of Pinetrees	15
Under Mount Charlotte	16
Dogleg Corner, Omimi	17
Graveyard Beach, Omimi	18
Above Boulder Beach	19
A Visit to Clifton House	20
From the Hut Window	22
Helicopter Ride / Cherry Farm	25

II
Music Therapy

Waiting Room (1)	30
The Art Class	31
Eye Ward	36
The Broken Houses	40
The Garden	42
Therapy over Carisbrook	43
Beach Therapy	44
Problem in the Therapy Room	45
Therapy in the Snow	46
A Game of Marbles	47
Waiting Room (2)	48
Music Therapy	49
Intermezzo	53
Execution of Karla	55

III
The Dead Woman's House

Night Fishing	58
One Morning on the Jetty	59
The Dead Woman's House	61
The Beachcomber	62
Bad Omokoroa	63
Anxiety on Onetangi Beach	64

I
Uncovering the Hospital

Letter from Seacliff

This Indian summer goes on.
Shall I tell you about it
over a bottle of port
in the light of a Chinese kerosine lamp
with the red lava-lava curtain billowing
in the breeze?

This is the first piece of writing I've done
for months –
so please bear with me . . .

Let me begin by telling you about the mice.
The tribe of mice that were here before I turned up
& drove them out.
It wasn't pretty.
I played this game.
I caught mice in a trap.
Most of the mice died instantly.
I pretended I had a Buddha nature
that I was above what was happening.
I pretended it was the trap that killed the mice
not me.
I kept setting the trap to prove the point.
Are they suicidal?
What's wrong with them?
Can't they see the danger?
I even left a candle burning
so they could see clearly what they were doing.
Finally they got the message & left.
I cleaned up the droppings. Pulled the paper
out of the walls.
Wiped up the blood.
The hut was mine.

Uncovering the Hospital

1

The weekend visitors who arrived with soft cheese
& french bread with hopes for field mushrooms

have gone home satisfied:
plastic bags full of plums & wild apples - stories

of madmen full of goat's head soup slitting
the throats of virgins - simple things

like chooks scratching in the compost
home-baked bread & elderberry wine

children being bitten by geese
the hut nearly blowing over in the night by gales

mice upside down in traps
squealing on the kitchen floor.

2

After the horizontal world of mad city
this vertical scene is driving me nuts.

I rig up a bamboo blind
across the hut window to chop through

the vertical lines of post, tree
& diving magpies, joining

the thin line of sea running from
macrocarpa on the right to the old

hospital mortuary hidden in hawthorn
shadow on the left.

3

All morning
the geese in the lower paddock
squabble & fight.
Nearing the end of autumn.
Already the smell of frost in the shade.

I fork around the marrow patch
feeding in some sheep droppings
gathered from under the pinetrees
above the hospital laundry.

To get there
you have to walk through what used to be
the female exercise enclosure, or what was
sometimes referred to as an airing court.

All that now remains is a concrete pad
where a shelter used to be, a plane tree
& a waterpipe sticking out of the ground
with a tap on the end of it surrounded by
sheep droppings & shards of wire reinforced glass.

4

Coming from across the road
the sounds of a work-gang kicking a ball
& laughing in their lunch-hour.

They're uncovering the hospital
preparing for weekend fungalists
& cuckoo watchers.

They're digging grass out of drains
planting flax in the enclosures
marigolds round the gate -
the gate with the cattle-stop.

5

Four eggs, a thermos flask
& one baby pumpkin
sit on the narrow windowsill of the hut.
Lying under the sleeping bag
with the window open at my feet
drinking coffee laced with brandy -
Van Morrison moon-dancing on the radio.

The impatient horses in the paddock
scrape & stomp expecting the promised cold rain
to sweep in from the west - autumn breeze
still warm. A mouse
runs suddenly up
the cloth-covered wall caught in
the flickering candle-light.

6

At cow gully swamp
buried under straw & blackcurrant
the remains of the old mental hospital -

you can't get away from it!

Galvanized steel
heavy netting
ventilation shoot
electric wire
electric bed!
fennel in bottomless chamber pot -

every piece of waxed floor
screw
lock
nut
accounted for.

Black & white cows
stumble dopily
through ragwort . . .

I attract little attention
as I carefully dig out
selected bricks
from the mortar & clay crumbling bank
to use to build a fireplace
in the hut.

7

Walking back to Seacliff from Evansdale
in my new oilskin & woollen singlet
on a cold & windy night
carrying in my pack a block of cheese
a bottle of McWilliams port 3 bananas
4 tomatoes 2 flat cans
of Canadian sardines & a new packet
of Park Drive tobacco tucked in with
some Sunday bacon . . .

Four wheels good, two legs bad
seems to be the motto round here.
The locals bump by in their trucks & vans
lighting up the hills & gullies
& my dark hooded sinister oilskin face
with their wobbly headlights
but don't stop.

What are they afraid of - lunatics?
Mad cows?
An aeroplane & satellite glide easily across the sky.

8

Long shadows in the middle of the day. Two magpies
balance & scrap on the tip of a tree - part
then fall like sheets of screwed up paper.
Geese cackle in a paddock out of sight.

9

Last night I woke to bloodcurdling screams
coming from somewhere in the yard.
I rushed out naked with torch flashing
in all directions, the sound confusingly
coming from everywhere at once.

I stood there
heart racing in the sudden silence
that follows a death-scream
cock shrivelled to nothing
torch shaking on cabbage & fencepost
seeing nothing
not wanting to see anything.

At first light I followed the feather trail
across the horse paddock
through the hawthorn hedge where I lost it
in blackberry . . .

It's not the first chook -
others have met the same fate
their bodies found under hedges
pulled up into trees bellies torn open
insides eaten out.

A ferret will do this because it has to kill
in the middle of the night when the surface
of the earth is quiet.
What's left we bury
in the spud patch.

10

Cold rain quietens the geese
drives them to shelter under the hedges
where I spread the kitchen scraps
for their nightly pecks.

During the recent frosty spell
they roamed restless morning & night
from field to field scratching
billing & maniacal cackling
as if looking for something special
& not finding it . . .

Gathering wood for fires
is a problem in this weather.
Hard to get anything to burn.
Everything covered in a thick layer
of fluffy down & goose-shit.

11

A spider crawls out of the end of a piece
of blazing wood & drops on its thread
to ash & pineneedles at the fire's hearth.

Unless something intervenes it is unlikely
to survive as the place it now finds itself
is almost as hot
as the place it evacuated . . .

12

For tea tonight I think I'll have
stuffed marrow
baked over a pinecone fire
in the new fireplace made with bricks
from cow gully swamp -

washed down
with ragwort wine.

The Superintendent's Garden

No patient's names
are carved on these trees
old mans beard
where names should be

Magnolia
crabapple
wild plum
names without stone

Those who walk on paths of ash
also play croquet
cut grass
work in the superintendent's garden
build bridges of stone
plant borders of red-hot pokers
drink tea in the pagoda sunshelter
watch trees burn

The trellis that holds up apple & vine
conceals a hospital wall
an unhappy magnolia
a mad bellbird
weaver of chicken wire . . .

In the superintendent's garden
the doctor & his wife are strolling -
he in stiff collar pipe & moustache
she in sunhat & scarf
hands clasped

The garden is a picture -
fat hydrangeas against
a white two-storied house
a sunporch that looks
like a box of dates
a clean path running down to bush
a large macrocarpa
at the back
the click of croquet balls

The doctor is looking into the pond
he's counting fish
remarks to his wife the size of the lily -
We'll put some more fern against that bank
maybe some netting to deter the cats
& look!
an unusual butterfly . . .

They stroll to the end of the Japanese path
in the shade of magnolia & wild plum
birdsong from behind a trellis of bees
bees without name

From a Grove of Pinetrees

Sitting here drinking thermos tea & writing this
after collecting pinecones in a place
(you'll appreciate) our forefathers would call
a God forsaken place!
Well the sheep seem to like it
but they scattered when I entered their domain.

Freezing squalls of fine hail swirl
through the grove & spiral up the sides
of the gigantic pinetrees
easily reaching the gaps
finding the hollow I crouch in.
Already the hills to the south are sprinkled with snow
the sky darkening early marking
the end of the Indian summer . . .

First I fill the backpack with pinecones
then a sack with chunks of wood & bark.
Must not make the load too heavy
it's a long way back to the hut.
                      How desolate
it is here.
The roar of the trees!
The mad frightened look on the faces of the sheep.

Then you notice it under the dark side of a tree
the one that didn't run with the others
dry coughing, jerky breathing
half lying in a nest of pineneedles.

Under Mount Charlotte

Sitting in a derelict tram
    at the Transport & Technology Museum
in the former Seacliff Mental Hospital
imagining riding home
after a hard day's work
reading a 1955 newspaper & casual glance out
the window & acknowledging my fellow passengers,
the ghosts of mental patients,
silent in
the whistling air. We share the same human,
possum, bird vandalized tram, dandelion tracks
running to nowhere -
the brightest blue sky.

So quiet outside as we go slow past the hospital cells
    & exercise yard,
shadows under veranda
could be bird-straw & paper
could be a man lighting another man's cigarette
someone waiting for a tram
could be an attendant, bare arms vice-like around something,
the doors of the cells slightly ajar revealing
sheets of leaves,
paper,
a flapping piece of curtain,
a meshed window.
Barely that.
Barely a movement or hint of anything
having lived here before
but straw . . .

We jolt to a stop in the middle of a godless patch
    of wild grass
under the shadow of Mount Charlotte -
'Are we home? Is this the end of the line?'
    my fellow passengers ask.
We step down onto the metal grates & drains of
    the exercise yard,
hesitant,
busting for a pee.

Dogleg Corner, Omimi

I remember walking back from Warrington
late one cold foggy night drunk on whisky
& bananas (for energy) aware of being
scared of vicious farm dogs & carrying
a big heavy stick for protection,
approaching Omimi railway crossing
where in the day time two or three
little grey dogs attempt to ravage
anything passing - including trains.

One limping yapper in particular
who seems to be leader of a pack called
the Barbed Wire Gang
charges fearlessly at anything that
doesn't resemble a hawthorn hedge.
Mad, one-eyed, scrawny-brained
hind leg dragging in the dust crooked
from some ancient clash - something
elusive, unavenged - religious.

I remember the gully below the crossing
where the road goes dark
smelling of frost & decay
dropping below the ragwort fields
into some childish fear of dark & bush
(the whisky not helping) & up the other side
feeling vaguely triumphant into more ragwort
& outlines of sheep not noticing
anything but the grass in front of them.

And when I arrived back safe to the hut
where I live with suicidal mice & vegetable
garden, I lit the kerosine lamp to try
to warm things up a bit. But it was hopeless.
The fog was too much into me.
The closeness of the hut made me nervous.
I had to make do with a cup of whisky & coffee
& a cold sleeping bag. The sound of mice
chewing under the floorboards.

Graveyard Beach, Omimi

These shells will break up become sand
& blow away
to be replaced by other shells
& oyster catchers . . .
Feather
sand
wave
rise as one
like sandflies.

And thousands of sandflies hover over
the smooth-worn cow dead in the rocks
skin blackened by salt & sun, goose eggs
laid in its bones its belly evaporated.
Two other fresh-dead cows fallen over
the cliff at night
legs broken, wedged in rocks.
One plucked goose stiffened in the
attitude of flight. Four ewes
dead from giving birth in a creek-slit
on the edge of the slippery shore.
Three paradise ducks circle the sky
their high-pitched calls mingling with
the sounds of thousands of sandflies.

I lie on my back in the tough cliff-grass
& listen to the waves far below
crash on the clay beach -
rain spitting on my face.
A good place to sleep.

Above Boulder Beach

After I left Boulder Beach & the dilapidated
boatshed with the one black gumboot (that some
one-legged fisherman is probably looking for)
I walked up a small gully till I came to a camp:
tin bivvy & chimney against overhanging rock
& bush. A haven for sheep - sheep droppings in
the not so old ash. A haven also for divers -
after the small juicy paua - & shooters who stalk
the feral geese that live in the area.

I walked on up the steep hill following sheep tracks
stopping to rest under some bent southerly-blown
trees, rolled a smoke, drank tea from the thermos
& took in the view of the splendid bay. Then moving on
to a hedge-enclosed paddock full of geese who
took off with a fantastic noise when I came into
sight - their throaty sounds curving over fields &
gully letting me know how pissed off they were . . .

And there, where some had been scratching in a
sheltered corner, lay a sheep on its side, just
alive & no more - its legs barely scraping the ground
where the grass had worn away, trying to right itself:
long shaggy wool, massive dags, doped eyes. Twice
I tried rolling it upright & twice it fell over, its
legs too weakened by days lying on flattened grass.

I had to leave it & walk on up a soggy gully back to
the coast road. And later, puffing from too many smokes
& warm nights, I paused high above where Boulder Beach
lay, & tracing my eye along the hedge-line to
the goose paddock, I could just see a small dot moving
ever so slightly in a yellowed corner.

A Visit to Clifton House

A dark night
the kind only Seacliff can give.
Gert & Volley (the German tourists) have moved
into Clifton House, partly as a dare
partly out of necessity for somewhere to sleep.

Armed with surplus-store stretcher, imagination
& kerosine lamp, Volley chooses not
to sleep in the upstairs cells but stays put
in the large sitting-room in a space where
a full-sized billiard table used to be. Builds
a blistering fire in the giant fireplace,
busys himself making billy tea
full of gothic apprehension.

Gert takes a corner double room lined with
wooden shelving & cupboards labeled
Psychiatric Notes
Drug Record
Medication.
Unpacks his sleeping bag candle stub & tobacco -
a man without fear
welcomes any visitor . . .

Built in 1917 to treat World War One
nerve cases
& looking more like a mountain chalet than
a hospital
it was later used as a convalescent home for
mental patients.
More recently
it has become a kind of backdrop to a past
that never was. A fantasy
of bricks & wire
possums & birdstraw
fruit peelings
dope parties
sunday tennis
a picnic place for the curious . . .

I feel my way down the dirt track
to see how the boys are doing
to share a smoke & cup of tea -
half-moon tearing through clouds
                      (cows bellowing)
a train running close blown closer by wind -
swaying long grass at the edge of the tennis court

gates strung with loose cattle wire.

From the Hut Window

      I

The black rooster
can't run for a tin of shit -
the hens get all the wheat

The rooster doesn't know
what's going on

. .

Yellow sun
on frost -
children chasing geese

      2

Fine rain
from the west

All day shut
in the hut -
wood fire
vegetable stew

cooked marrow
cooling
for the impatient chooks

3

Lying here watching insects
through the bamboo blind
zigzag across
the window pane

fine rain

. .

The faces of cattle
wide as landscapes

Flat white beasts
hair parted
neatly in the middle

like sheepskin rugs
in front of fireplaces

4

The grey horse
takes enormous
careful mouthfuls
of green thistle -

balances his body
against the chicken-wire fence

. .

Cows have cut loose
on the hospital grounds

A green bird
white on either side of its tail
sits on a wire
its belly puffed out

Half concealed in hawthorn
the mortuary
looms out of the mist

. .

Fog & geese
float across the paddock -

an audience of shabby fenceposts

    5

Spring & mist
run up & down
the grass stalks -

stray flowers wander
across the road

Trees printed on sea -
a container ship moving
through trees

. .

From the hut window
I see a horse drop
a steamy morning turd -

delightful!

Helicopter Ride/
Cherry Farm

Gala day
& the young girls folkdancing on the lawn
are as sweet as multiheaded spiders -
gypsy skirts & limbs like blades . . .

Nothing had changed
not even the chapel.

The recreation hall where we once
had our morning O.T. physical jerks
after breakfast & chlorpromazine
& sometimes dizzy dancing with a cheerful
toothy gramophone, hearts thumping like
boards hitting flesh
still the same.
The same black piano behind
the same stage curtain -

the same agoraphobic lawn.

The soggy bowling green
& nurses quarters
& villas with their weedy gardens
around the big doors,
prim
neat
proper,
still the same.

'9' & 'H'
down the hill
tucked out of sight
full of bad vibes
cold
(better forgotten)
the same . . .

Apples
balloons.
A slow blue & white merry-go-round.
Some amplified jingle.

When the wooden ball hits the target
a man in a clown suit
falls into a vat of water
(or snake oil).
A slow blue & white merry-go-round.

The girls folkdancing on the grass
in brightly coloured skirts
spin faster
& faster
a whirlpool of straw, hair & eyes.

The superintendent of the hospital
ritually burning on a bonfire
signs that say
Schizophrenia
Depression
Hysteria
amid carefree applause.
They chant as the smoke spirals skyward
Burn the myth!
Kill the monster!
Ash to ash!
The black flames leap higher.

In a tent erected
on the edge of agoraphobia
a former charge nurse
takes Devonshire tea
mingles with the people
reads palms eyes
head-size - can predict
the future. Has published
a small pamphlet on the history
of the hospital.
Admits recklessly
to damaged memory
(I need a shot of electricity)
- helps himself to a cream-cake
topped with a cherry.
And we the visitors the ex-inmates
file past to see
a demonstration
on how to restrain
an unloved person . . .

A helicopter lifts off the shaky lawn
(ten dollars a ride)
with a clatter-bang of hot air
& screams
(someone's left on the ground kicking)
& wheels up
up
like an unhinged merry-go-round -

up over the pines
the empty chapel
the sewer pipes
the creek where we caught eels -

high over
the clay of Karitane
the boulders of Seacliff
the blue of Blueskin Bay -

over cabbage & rhubarb
your home
& mine
& those who look up from their gardens
dumbfounded
at the queer
clattering in the sky.

II
Music Therapy

Waiting Room   (I)
(notebook entry)

Moths on the electric
clock's face animate

Ambiguous outlines
only plate glass hydrangeas

- ENQUIRIES
He should not be long
he will not be very long

Pot plants this time of the year
are lovely
aren't they?

A little treatment
will do you the world of good
the world of good

See
it's not so bad after all
is it . . .

March fairies
rolling across the scuffed waiting room floor

That magazine
I've read it before

The Art Class

    I

A jostling for the best light
A pastel panorama of ocean waves

Glimpses of bathers holding hands underwater
Exaggerated hairstyles, breasts, eyes

Dolphins in rooms without exits
Pick your own flowers

    2

'T' up-ends a pot of black paint on her paper
smearing the entire surface with it, pushing the paint

outwards to the corners with a thick
brush, then with another

slaps a big rough pair of wet red lips
smack in the center

then with white yellow-streaked paint
writes R.I.P. on the top

then folds it up still wet
smaller & smaller till it's gone

. . .

'J' paints scissors blood & eyeless masks
dangling in space, neatly separated like

houses & letterboxes or water
& bather . . . but 'L' goes
one step further & draws a small stout

tree chopped off about head height without
leaves or branches
surrounded by wide white sky,
then sits for the rest of the period feet up

arms tight round knees
nose & hair buried in thighs

her small body
filling the room

    3

Walking home after therapy
I call into my old pub
for a glass of lemon squash
& of course to see who's
hanging round.
The TV's on high in the corner
over the pooltable. The midday news
from someplace where it's still night.
Something terrible's happening.
There's a man with a gasmask on
talking into a microphone - behind him
in a window a city
dark with uncertain lights flashing.
Now & again movements in the sky.
It's a mad painting
or a trick of dream.
The man in the mask could be seconds
from dying for all we know . . . but there's
only a muffled voice
on & on 'missile war gas'

& a dark long-legged girl
with a tattoo of a butterfly
on her calf
smiling cross-eyed
waiting for her turn on the table

. . .

There are no people in these pictures.
One has a building with an airshaft in the middle
another has a bomb going down an airshaft
& another has smoke like burning oil

spewing everywhere out of an airshaft
with walls dissolving & starlike explosions
appearing & disappearing as the paint
brush moves across the surface in smudges
of yellow & white . . .

'N's' target looks like a breast
with a neat round dot
in the middle.
-What is it? we ask
& he stares at it long & hard
but says nothing.
But we know quite well what it is.
It is a cottage with a smoking chimney,
a spiral or church spire like snails
or dolphins that lead to
nirvana

    4

In a vase you arrange your subject:
something between the object of your imagination
& light.
You allow your thoughts to move along quickly
at random - choosing first
the black over blue
till the black's used up & the blue isn't blue
anymore

& you have to change the water
in the jam-jar till it's bubbly clear (enough
for a tadpole to swim in)
then look for another colour - like that
on the edge of a feather.
   What happens
in the end more often than not
is a lovely mess
& a disturbed construction:
too much black
too much merging . . .
For a moment
you become an expert in an existence
that lies between
two things:
vague figures skating on ice in a school yard,
comic houses standing on sugar-cake hill,
crepe flowers in a waterless vase,
scissors cutting air

   5

We hear the news
'S' died by drowning in seawater

There was a hiatus.
We knew.
We waited.
There were sightings.
Personal items.
An urgent orderly biographical detail
in the newspaper.
Something settling on the beach . . .

She leaves behind
lipstick,
an unfinished papier mache mask,
a photograph
one less breath -
'On the road to nowhere'
'I'm dead'

6

The painting hangs in the room with no exits.
Pastel-smooth with
dark flowing hair.
Hands neatly folded
in an attitude
of meditation.
Eyes half closed

We all agree
she looks happy

she worked hard

Eye Ward

Japanese garden full of unmoving waves
room of shadows
room of sand

I am here
to have my eye operated on
to have the sight restored to my left eye
to have my eye terrorized
made to work
like it was supposed to work -
not look left when told to look right
but track one with the other
like the yellow headlights of a car
skidding on ice

The Japanese garden is for the eye patients
a calming picture of serenity
& coolness.
One can stand in the corridor hum
of the air-conditioned hospital
& wet a nose on the reflecting glass
that separates this air from that
& watch endless imaginary waves crash onto
finely raked sand
& recall
faint salt dreams . . .

The anaesthetist calls
wants to measure me up
take my weight
explain the procedure of execution:
there'll be 3 pink pills (for nerves)
nil per mouth after midnight
no smoking
& do you have your own teeth?
sign here
you may have to give some blood

I am here
to have my eye operated on.
Cut

A man with a trolley
appears
I'm lying on it.
We wheel down
the smoothest longest
darkest passage in the world
(the universe)
past the scary rubber-plants
the paintings of clouds
& egg-shells
like eye-balls
on the wall
by the lift
the tilting lift
the toothless lift

I'm frightened.
The lift goes up
not down.
Something's happened to my legs
they're missing.
The man smiles.
The lift is humming like a refrigerator.
A misty wave breaks over eggs.
We lurch violently to the left.
We lurch violently to the right.
There is a shouting
of names
an aching light
an accusation
a pointing
a finger in the eye . . .

The family of the man in the bed
opposite me
are visiting.
They present the man with a cake
full of fruit.
The left side of his face is
heavily bandaged.
Bits of white hair stick out
the edges.
He's lying back almost slipping off
a huge pile
of pillows
& they're telling him
It's good to see you looking
so well Jack
sit up, you're slipping -
the river didn't flood
after all
the cows are fine
the hens are laying
can you see yet?
what's the food like?
& when do they say you can come home?

The specialist appears.
The examination will be short.
How many fingers? he says
confidently
in a clear accent
holding up his hand
in front of my face.
All I can see
out of my new eye
are 2 goldfish in a bowl
of dirty water
with a bit of bloody weed
floating
in the middle -
Five (I guess
to be on the safe side)

Three,
you're not bad -
don't forget the drops
you can go home

I watch him out of my good eye
through the ward window
walk round the corner
into the corridor
past the Japanese garden
without stopping
till he's out
of sight

The Broken Houses
(for Heather)

You guard one end of the street
& I the other.
No one or thing escapes our notice -
cats, trespassing children
unidentified lights
unclaimed mail.

The elderly neighbours
locked in their flats
with leg-sores & blinking television
need our watching,
the noisy people in the two storied houses
at the end of the cul-de-sac
forever partying
driving their rowdy cars fast up & down
the street like they own it
need our watching,
the marijuana dealer (we won't mention
his name) & the policecar that screams up
the street on Thursday nights
need our watching,
the church people over the hedge in the big house
where they run the food bank
always busy doing something
never stopping to say hello
need our watching,
the broken houses of the abandoned farm
behind the golf-course
overlooking Blackhead & wild southern ocean
(where you were once frightened by bluegums)
need our watching . . .

I come to your flat at night
when the street is quiet
to watch TV, to share a biscuit & thought -
'What did you have for tea tonight?'
'Did you go for a walk this afternoon?'
'How was therapy?'

I don't stay long
I never do -
I'm like a child
running across your lawn
chasing unidentified lights.

The Garden

Last night an ambulance took away the man & woman
from across the road
down to the city of lights & harbour
its own lights revolving slowly
so as not to give the impression of haste.
One stood & looked for a while at the space
across the footpath where the ambulance had stood
half in half out of the garden
its back doors flung open sucked into dark.

Today the woman is back moving stiffly between shrubs
looking for something: a flower, a twig of green
a piece of fern to make up a posy
then, slightly hunched moves quickly
out of the bitter nor-east wind back to the house
her neat grey hair darting like a bird . . .

I take my spade to the old rose bush in front of my flat.
It has been lately attracting too many wasps.
The trap I made from a honey pot with pieces
of rotted fruit & vinegar worked well - I must
have caught hundreds - yet they keep coming
from God knows where.
I'll replace the bush with something else
something the wasps won't like.

There's a hole where the rose bush used to be.
I guess the man across the road will not be back
to mow the grass verge along the fence.
Every morning
the woman gathers a few things from the garden
backs her yellow car out of the drive
& rolls off toward town - down into the dark
glistening harbour.

Therapy over Carisbrook

Above where I live helicopters fly.
They skim the tops of old macrocarpas
& drop with obscene clattering down the hill
to hover rudely above the flying-saucer shaped
football field.
Forty-thousand rugby fans scream
blue murder as a lady in pink tights &
yellow parachute leaps out of an eggbeater.
As she hits the ground the comedy begins.
The helicopter reappears somewhere above
where I live shaving another branch off a tree . . .
  If you fly hot-air balloons you must obey
traffic signals & watch for bad weather
& helicopters.
Cows may jump over moons,
swimmers may float for some time in freezing
water - addicts drown (temporarily)
& come back to life again - one may even
develop the art of walking on water, depending
on one's state of mind at the time - but watch
for thin ice . . . nothing can save you
from thin ice.

Beach Therapy

Sitting in these hokey pokey sandhills
eating fish & chips
watching the bright vanilla waves roll in to
the kelp-strewn beach.

A black dog like a seal in the hazy
distance playing with a stick - a man
in a checked shirt trying to run hard
backwards up a sandhill - the late sun

slanting through cloud above the coast hills
& three dots running on stick legs away
from the hurrying foam, lifting
& becoming sharp wing-like things

climbing high above marram grass & hazy sun
then diving suddenly screeching ghastly
where I throw a chip.
And at the foam's edge the black dog
lies panting
its tongue hanging out, stuffed.

Problem in the Therapy Room

I can't seem to write anything today
I've got red on the brain
I keep thinking of a dream I had
of a baby in a pram outside a coffee bar

Its mother was talking with a man
a stranger?
The baby looked from face to face
from leg to leg
its own face growing redder

They're talking about it
discussing its problem
imagined or otherwise
fitting it out for a future
which school to send it to
who will bring it up

The woman bends down to adjust the red blanket
around the baby's legs
(the wind is cold)
when she straightens up
the man is gone.

Therapy in the Snow

Sparrows and waxeyes feed on the bread
I throw in the snow from my back doorway -
The flax I planted not so long ago
bends under the weight of snow
but does not move when a waxeye
                         alights on it -
Darting like bumblebees they must keep moving
lest they die or freeze - It is polite
to take a beak-full of crumb
& flit away quickly to make room
                         for someone else -
Chaos reigns briefly when a young
spotted starling materializes -
A row of green buds appear on the flaxbush -
Suddenly the snow becomes bare:
the neighbour's cat has crossed the road
                         to investigate -
Only tiny footmarks remain.

A Game of Marbles

The big boys ran the game.
The ones who had the most marbles were king.
These were kept in a cotton bag that hung
from the belt like a prized scalp.

The town I grew up in was full of churches.
That's what I think of when I think of marbles.
There was the favoured bloodeye, a clean glass marble
with a centre-shot of red like a piece
of hair suspended in space
or a church spire against sky.
Clay marbles were not so valued
because they were small & old & very plentiful
& looked like the brick walls of school.

You won an opponent's marble by knocking it
out of a circle carefully drawn with a stick
in the dirt at the back of the school dunny
    with one of your own.
Naturally, the small boys had few to lose.
There was no protection.
You made your hole in the dirt between the clumps
    of grass & played.
You played because you had to.
You went to church because you had to.

The minister looked down from the pulpit
& fixed his bloodeye on the top of your head.
You squirmed in the pew.
Fiddled with your hymn book.
The sermon was always about his people
    big & small.
Bloodeyes & clays. The size of your bag.
Like spuds pumpkins & cabbages
on harvest festival days -
share with your neighbour
be thankful for small mercys
& forgive those who act like magpies.

Waiting Room   (2)

Endless tap of typewriter & buzzing phone.
Rag doll. Commercial radio. Loud speaker high
on wall.
Picture of retired Superintendent.
One huge rubber plant.
Doctor fifteen minutes late.

- SUNDAY, VISITING DAY
I remember when you first came to see me
at the Farm. We went for a walk to the river.
(I still had freedom of movement then)
You lay on the bank in your tight striped pants
in the daisy grass two feet from the dark green water
& looked up at my scared white face.
We had to walk quickly back to the Villa.

The horrible dry mouth. The stupid sense
I was only a visitor myself. How else could I
smell the river?
Those ones in the tennis court sitting on stools
in the sun in badly fitting tennis shoes were not
playing tennis.
And we were on this side of the high thick netting
walking on the gravel path, smoking.

- NOTEBOOK ENTRY
Alone in the waiting room
a girl with thin arms & face
plays with car keys, lights cigarette,
crosses uncrosses legs, glances at
rubber plant. Nervous fiddle with handbag . . .

Out of the tap tap wall
a nurse appears - clipboard &
slippered feet. Takes girl away
quickly
into the hospital's dry mouth.

Music Therapy

1

The old man in the bar
lights a cigarette
squeezes the ember between
finger & thumb
(beer & rum)
spider-plant eyebrows
long elegant fingertips
criss-cross
the smoky air.

Thin grey hair
long down neck
curling behind ears
snotty moustache
stubby jaw
berry nose -
grimaces as he crosses
his legs . . .

2

Pick out a song
or track
from the pile of old records
on the coffee table

that may or may not match
a feeling or mood you have
about yourself
or someone else

that you might like to play
on the stereo
& share with another person
in the group.

3

Walking through town this morning
on my way to the hospital
I was surprised by the amount
of white in everything. For instance
the people with their white eyes &
smiles & the white fumes
of the traffic
surrounded by the bright colours
of the new windowless department stores -
my brain having no trouble
taking it all in despite
the medication & my silly feeling . . .
Till I saw an elegant woman
in a sleek black outfit
& broad red scarf around her neck
standing in the middle of the footpath
looking into a shop window
at a dummy in evening clothes
& identical red scarf - dazzled
with reflections of white.
And I wanted to reach out
& touch the red scarf
but I knew I couldn't.

4

Trees are like music.
After the gathering of leaves,
a silence.

No one has to talk
if they don't want to
the therapist says . . .

When the needle finds the groove
there's an awkward hiss, like blood,
like sex.
We remember
though we don't want to remember.

5

I'm afraid I won't be able to do
this exercise.
I can't help it if I can't remember.

My lips hurt.
So do my fingers.
How am I expected to play this thing
if my fingers hurt?

I've told you everything I know
about my family.
The cold rooms.
Prayer.
Work.
The stick on the backside.

Maybe there's a song for it
I don't know what.
I can't tell you.
I would if I could.

6

We sit on the lawn
under the trees
& watch the people
walk back & forth
in front of the hospital.

No one talks
there's nothing to say
but watch the cars
go back & forth
in front of the hospital . . .

7

Upstairs in a room where we play our songs
they're screaming
boiling water
making milo
separating dancers.

And bouncing on cushions
with an overstuffed teddybear
there's one with a face like
watery paper

laughing
falling
letting go

milo flying everywhere.

Intermezzo

Once I met this queen
who bought me a hamburger
in a late night coffee bar . . .

I was lonely with nowhere to go.
I wandered the streets day & night
looking for places to sleep
& places where I could get something to eat.
Sometimes I met up with desperadoes
who were hiding from the police.
Small-time thieves, runaways,
homeless they took me to old abandoned
buildings where they lived with
newspapers & bottles.
There we shared a laugh a story
a lit candle
& when we got hungry we wandered down town
to the all night coffee bars to chat up
the queens & butch coffee bar owners.
If you were quick you could do
a bit of dishwashing out the back
for a cup of coffee & toasted sandwich
& sometimes you got a bit of something else
if the coffee bar owner liked you.
Nobody minded if you were square
nobody asked how old you were
nobody cared if you stayed all night
nobody asked what your father did.
Sometimes the police came in looking
for someone.
They would push you against the wall
with the queens & bring their knee up
where it hurts,
but they rarely hurt.
There was a kind of laughter in their eyes.

Sometimes a cop would see someone
he recognized & drag them outside into
the street & there would be the sound
of rubbish bins flying
& shouting
though no one took much notice.
It was like they were king & you
were there for them to play with.
Like they were bored.

And once I went for a ride
in a car with a queen called Passionfruit
up the Kapiti Coast
but we didn't do anything
we just sat there smoking
being quiet
watching the sun go into the sea
then we drove back to sleep
in a crap rooming-house
behind Wellington Cathedral . . .
I can still see the piles of
make-up jars & pill bottles
in that half-cold room.

This was 1966
& nobody cared what you looked like,
whether you had any money or not
so long as you kept off the streets.
If you wanted a feed
you only had to ask.
If you wanted someone to talk to
you sat quietly till someone appeared.
And if you were lucky
you got some cigarettes
& someone else to sleep with.

Execution of Karla

Anytime soon
    (as the parlance goes)
    they'll offer you a happy pill
    (which you'll turn down)
    they'll fit you out in a white gown
    measure your arm
    check for the vein
    (some veins are hard to find) -
    & while you're practicing being brave & angelic
    I'll be walking home from the therapist's in a bad mood
    & while you're consciously removing all trace
    of prison hygiene & pain from your face
    & you're approaching the cross-shaped bed you'll lie on
    for eternity
    I'll be in my garden hacking at weeds
    & stubborn new growth - I'll be helping
    my neighbour prepare a new flower-bed
    beneath the wash-house window:
    daisies ferns large & tall
    & you'll be lying there
    on the cross-bed
    dark curly hair
    a lost star
    eyes fixed on God.

But you'll see only murdered faces
    & a pick axe -
    no God, Karla - no suddenly through a glass clearly
    no meaning of life
    only a million television screens
    only the human blood in the ears
    like a burst pipe -
& I will water the new garden as well as I can
    this dry weather:
    how dry it's been!
    the grass so brown
    the plants are in trouble
    & you'll be dead
    your face will have lost recognition.

They'll leave you there for a while
    out of respect.
    They'll take the tube out of your arm
    & fold your hands.
    They'll close the Bible on the passage
    you marked.
    One last look at your bright curly hair.

What's it like Karla?
    Is death worse than death now?
    do you see the faces of the suicides
    the o.d.'s the hangmen
    with quaint English voices the hangmen
    with quaint American voices?
    are there any clergymen there Karla?

The rubbish-man came today
    athletically leaping in & out of the shiny
    truck's cab
    & with a deft flick of the wrist
    (as the parlance goes)
    he removed my guilt
    my tidy bag disappearing into the yawning
    mouth of eternity . . .
    My therapist would advise, Let it go -
    put it behind you . . .

III
The Dead Woman's House

Night Fishing

Full moon off
pipi point
writing this
with coat hood up

sound of train
in the dark
slippery mud
pontoon blood

on the jetty
night fishing
sound of men
laughing

plastic bucket
brighter eyes
crabs' fingers
climbing lines

wet black wood
yellow light
over there
a wading bird

shrill calls
above light
up there
beyond night

sudden yell
in the dark
something there
something caught

ghostly laughter
colder wind
sound of water
going home.

One Morning on the Jetty

1

Wally is so deaf
the barge
when bearing on the jetty
has to sound several sharp blasts of its horn
to give him time to retrieve his line
before the barge runs over it.

On all sides
gannets dive for herring, hitting the water
like cannon-balls.

Wapiti, Wally's ancient ragged dog
half blinded by cataracts
lies exhausted on the pontoon licking
at pools of dried blood where last night's
fish have been gutted.

2

With his bucket of salted pipi
old Jack - the minister of Ag & Fish -
has been up since dawn, line out,
scrunty eyes scrutinizing the current.
Was a cook in Egypt during the war,
has driven cattle by horse-back along narrow bush tracks
that are now part of the town's main roadways.
Doesn't say much
but there isn't much he doesn't know about fish
land & sea -
You pickle herring, he says,
in vinegar & onion,
best eaten with white bread washed down
with strong black tea . . .
I don't understand why men
don't like the land anymore . . .

3

We wait for the hopeful bend of rod,
the alarming tick of reel.

4

A fizzboat breaks the tension
pulling in from Matakana Island.

A priest staggers off in his black
priest clothes clutching a guitar
looking the worse for wear. The boat

doesn't stop for conversation
speeds off in a wild curve like a soapy bullet
toward the shimmering mudbank . . .

Sometimes at night the mackerel
are so thick on the water
you could walk on them.

5

The stringy boys who come down to dive off the highest
poles like gannets
blow screams at each other under water -
are not afraid of bad-tempered men
are not changed by water.

6

Sometimes in the early morning at slack tide
when you see the back of the stingray
arching under pale light

kingfish come.

The Dead Woman's House

The last time I saw her (she being
practically blind & threequarters deaf) she was
watering her garden, hosing down the concrete path.
Now the lawn (neglected since her death) in places
is nearly a foot high
& the pansy garden-patch, concrete-block bordered,
stands bone-dry with weeds like dark tobacco
spreading across the chalky ground.
The white cat (once her constant companion) still
roams the property,
feeds on herring dropped by thoughtful locals returning
from night fishing at the jetty.
Late at night you'll see her under the yellow
street light
in front of the dead woman's house
sitting on a warm patch in the middle of the road,
silent, looking into the dark where everything moves,
then padding over
to where the fish are dropped
drooling saliva & meowing softly.

The Beachcomber

All night the storm blew,
masts, anchor-ropes crossed
buckets clattered across decks
voices whined from rigging to shore:
crabs upside down
shags drying in the sun

In the suburban mangroves
the beachcomber is alone:
senses his weight on unstable mud,
is aware of uncontrolled golfballs
the shadow of the black gull
the anxious slant of sun

Hopes of finding his face in sand
a corner of paradise
are shattered:
a farting fizzboat like a surfacing submarine
guns blazing
grinds up the greasy channel . . .

Smoke from fat rubbish fires
toward Mount Maunganui obscure
a dark helicopter:
two feet above mud a squawking heron floats away
like a flounder, a swarm
of tiny blue butterflies

Hopes of finding a corpse wedged
between rocks, mouth full of bright gold
fade:
some thin bones are all, & a cat
stiff
its eyes looking out at sea

Bad Omokoroa

Walking past the place where Mrs D
was smashed to death by a speeding car
as she crossed the road to check her letterbox.
A pheasant breaks loudly from
the avocado, flies out of sight
behind a hedge of feijoa.
A blue heron circles the sky.
Pukeko scatter from a vegetable plot . . .

The new houses going up around here are
(one must admit) beautiful specimens
of engineering & design. Any self-respecting
pheasant or heron would be glad to be seen
decorating these lawns. But they'll have
to carry guns under their wings, perhaps
know a bit of self-defence,
for the wily pukeko is not to be trusted.

The sport around here when driving down
these roads is to aim
for anything that doesn't have wheels -
hitch-hikers
hedgehogs
pukeko
anyone who can't say 'I like it' (with conviction)
when asked what they think of this place,
daydreamers mistaking the retirement village
for paradise,
anyone who doesn't shoot straight . . .

If I were the heron I'd stay in the sky
& leave bad Omokoroa to the land agents,
pukeko
& God.

Anxiety on Onetangi Beach

Another nuclear explosion in the city.
The temperature jumps from 25 to 2000 deg. C.
A windowdresser covers a dummy
with a thin veil.
Silky stretch of clean white sand
wind in the punga.

Sandals, beachbag
Christmas Humphreys' Zen, a Way
of Life,
expensive sunglasses,
two busloads of elderly beachcombers
up from Feijoa Country Estate for the day
browsing along the shoreline.
Bathe only between flags
the sign says.

A fleet of towtrucks
pulls into Onetangi garden tavern,
arrival of the carwrecker's annual get-together.
Hairless men & toothpick women
in skin & leathers
erect their tent between beach flags -
We fuck anything that moves.
The sea is a mass of vibrating radiators
& dismembered elderly . . .

When the pupil is ready
the master appears.
I open my eyes expecting to see
my ex-psychiatrist standing waist-deep
in Freudian-foam shouting
Castration anxiety!
but instead I see a man & a woman
& a small fluffy dog
playing in the surf -
children squealing in the waves
a collapsed sand mermaid dressed
in seaweed & shells
the smell of chilli sausage.

The moment passes.
The glass is cleared away
& the elderly go home in a fern-covered bus
chanting like Lunatics.
Christmas Humphreys is put aside.
One rips the beachbag apart searching
for the emergency pills,
lies gingerly back on the blazing sand
& listens to the morphine sounds
of AKA singing Free Nelson Mandela
on the personal stereo.

The holiday begins.